Presented To

Connor David Karl

— Dedicated to God —

Date

November 30, 2014

with love,
Gramma Sue

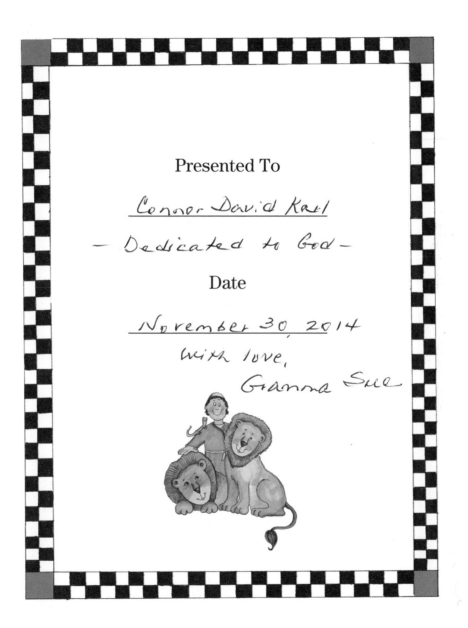

for
Mothers and Sons

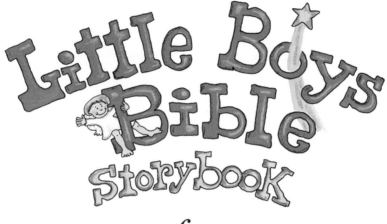

Little Boys Bible Storybook

for
Mothers and Sons

Carolyn Larsen
Illustrated by Caron Turk

BakerBooks

a division of Baker Publishing Group
Grand Rapids, Michigan

Text © 1999, 2014 by Carolyn Larsen
Illustrations © 1999 by Caron Turk

Published by Baker Books
a division of Baker Publishing Group
P.O. Box 6287, Grand Rapids, MI 49516-6287
www.bakerbooks.com

Printed in China

Library of Congress Cataloging-in-Publication Data
Larsen, Carolyn, 1950-
    Little boys Bible storybook for mothers and sons / Carolyn Larsen; illustrated by Caron Turk.
        pages   cm
    ISBN 978-0-8010-1546-5
    1. Bible stories, English. I. Turk, Caron, illustrator. II. Title.
BS551.3.L3697 2013
220.95′05—dc23   2013007615

Scripture quotations are from God's Word®. © 1995 God's Word to the Nations. Used by permission of Baker Publishing Group.

14   15   16   17   18   19   20   7   6   5   4   3   2   1

Contents

Dear Moms,

I had two daughters before my son was born. I remember people saying, "Boys are so different from girls; you'll see!" I didn't believe them because one of my daughters was an absolute daredevil and I didn't see how a boy could be any more energetic than she was. However, they were right. It's hard to explain how—but boys are definitely different to raise than girls are. That's why Caron Turk and I have tried to make this book a little more active, maybe a little more "rough-and-tumble" than the Little Girls Bible Storybook.

We hope the stories and illustrations in this book provide a chance for you and your son to see into the hearts of some well-loved Bible characters. Of course, we don't really know what those people actually felt or how they approached some of the situations they were in, but by thinking about what they may have felt, we can under-

stand some of the lessons they learned from their experiences. We hope this book helps your son realize that these were real people with problems, joys, successes, and failures—people like us!

Caron has created a spunky little boy angel who is hiding in every illustration. Often, his buddy, a little daredevil lizard, is with him. You and your son will have fun looking for the two of them.

My hope is that this book will bring familiar Bible stories to life for you and your son, and that the questions and thoughts in the Becoming a Man of God section will be good conversation starters for the two of you. I'm sure your son will love hearing about your childhood memories and experiences.

God bless you and your son as you read the Little Boys Bible Storybook for Mothers and Sons.

Carolyn Larsen

That's What Little Boys Are Made Of

Genesis 1–2

A brown bear scooped honey into his mouth, but when the ground began to shake, he dove behind a rock, peeking out at the swirling dust. God himself was moving the dirt! He was shaping it into his best creation—Adam, the very first man.

Adam stretched his arms and wiggled his fingers. He raced through the garden, checking out everything God had made for him. He skipped stones across a lake. He climbed a tree and hung upside down.

But a while later Adam slumped on the ground. "What's the matter, Adam?" God asked.

"I'm bored," Adam said with a sigh.

"Well, would you like to name the animals?" God asked. "They all need names. You can decide what to call each one." So Adam made up names for each one. But when he finished, he plopped down on the ground again.

"I know what the problem is," God said. "You're lonely. You need someone to talk with and do things with. Someone who is more like you than the animals." God made Adam fall asleep. He took one of Adam's ribs and used it to make Eve, the first woman.

You will be best friends..... ♥

"Wake up now," God whispered. Adam opened his eyes and saw a brand-new creature. "This is Eve," God said. "I made her to be your wife. You both are a lot like me—you can think, and talk, make decisions, and work together. I know you'll be very happy."

Becoming a Man of God

*A man of God knows he is made
in God's image.*

Adam and Eve were made in God's image. God made them to be like him. You are also made in God's image.

God is loving, kind, honest, and fair. So you should also be loving, kind, honest, and fair.

A Verse to Remember

As all of us reflect the Lord's glory with faces that are not covered with veils, we are being changed into his image with ever-increasing glory. This comes from the Lord, who is the Spirit.

2 Corinthians 3:18

At First Bite

"Adam!" Eve's voice blasted through the quiet garden. Adam could hear her running and stumbling over bushes.

"Over here, Eve," he called. He stepped out from behind a bush just in time for Eve to crash into him. "What's wrong?" he asked.

"Taste this—it's great!" Eve said, holding out a half-eaten piece of fruit.

Adam's breath caught in his throat. "That's from the tree God said not to eat from, Eve. He said if we even so much as touch it we'll die."

Adam recognized the fruit because he often wondered why God didn't want him to touch it. Eve had broken the only rule God gave them.

"We won't die," Eve said. "That snake over there said eating this fruit would make us more like God."

Adam knew he should just walk away, but the fruit smelled so sweet. Suddenly he grabbed it and took a big bite.

Right away Adam felt sad because he knew he had broken God's rule.

When God came to the garden later, Adam hid from him. God knew something was wrong. "Adam, what have you done?" he asked.

Adam tried to put the blame on Eve. But there was no way out of this. They had disobeyed.

"I have to punish you," God said sadly, "but remember that I still love you. I will always love you."

Becoming a Man of God

*A man of God takes responsibility
for his sin.*

Adam and Eve were made in God's image. But they could choose to obey or not to obey. In this story, they made a bad choice—they sinned— and God punished them.

We all sin—even if we try hard not to, we do. When was a time that you did something wrong?

A Verse to Remember

Though your sins are bright red
    they will become as white as snow.
Though they are dark red,
    they will become as white as wool.

Isaiah 1:18

Dad's Little Helpers

Genesis 6:1–7:9

"Boys, it's time to get up." Shem, Ham, and Japheth sat up and rubbed the sleep from their eyes.

As the boys sat down for breakfast, their mother said, "We have work to do. We're all helping your father build an ark because God told him to. We're obeying God."

Just then Noah came in. "That's right. God is tired of the way people are behaving. No one pays any attention to him anymore."

"Yeah, so God is going to wipe out the whole world with a big flood," Ham said. He stood on his chair and pretended to jump into water.

"This is not a joke," his mother said sternly. "God will save us because your father has led our family to obey God."

Soon the whole family was out in the yard. Each one had a job to do. Shem brought the wood, Ham carried buckets of tar, and Japheth smeared the tar on the boards.

Day after day, year after year, the whole family worked. By the time the ark was finished, the boys were grown up and married.

One day after the ark was finished, Japheth came running into the house. "Father, there are hundreds of animals headed this way! What do we do?"

"Open the ark and let them in," Noah answered.

The Noah family followed the animals into the ark and the rain began to fall.

Becoming a Man of God

A man of God obeys God.

Noah's sons were blessed to grow up in a family that honored and respected God. They knew that their father and mother lived for God and obeyed him. They learned to do the same.

When was a time you found it hard to obey? Why didn't you want to? What happened?

A Verse to Remember

If you love me, you will obey my commandments.

John 14:15

Too Much Togetherness

Genesis 7:1–9:17

At first Noah's sons thought it was a great adventure to be in the big boat. They fed the animals and played with them. All the while rain pelted the boat.

One morning Shem told Ham, "It's your turn to clean the cages."

"No way; I did it yesterday. It's Japheth's turn."

"Stop quarreling!" Mrs. Noah said.

"It's been raining for thirty days," Shem said. "Is it ever going to stop? Every day we wake up to the same old thing—feed the animals, clean the boat, listen to the rain. We want out of this boat."

About ten days later Japheth woke everyone up. "Hey! Do you hear that?"

"I don't hear anything," Shem said.

"I know. Isn't it great? The rain stopped. It's quiet."

"Let's get out of this boat!" Ham shouted.

"Slow down," Noah cautioned. "The water is still pretty deep out there."

When Noah finally said it was safe to leave, everyone cheered.

After they left the boat they saw a beautiful, shimmering arc of bright colors stretching across the sky.

For I will see the rainbow in the cloud and remember my eternal promise to every living being on the earth.

"This rainbow shows my promise to never destroy the world in a big flood again," God explained. "Every time you see a rainbow, remember how much I love you."

Noah prayed, "Thank you for saving us, God, and thank you for your promise."

Becoming a Man of God

A man of God remembers to thank God.

When Noah and his family stepped off the big boat, the first thing they did was thank God. We often ask God for things, and we must remember to thank him for answering our prayers.

When you help someone do you like to be thanked? Do you remember to thank God?

A Verse to Remember

Give thanks to the LORD because he is good, because his mercy endures forever.

1 Chronicles 16:34

The Miracle Baby

Genesis 18:1–15; 21:1–7

It sure is hot today, Abraham thought, sitting in the shade of a tree. Sarah was working inside their tent, stirring up treats for the children who would drop by later. Abraham and Sarah loved children, but they didn't have any of their own.

Abraham looked up and saw three men walking across the desert toward him. "Come sit here in the shade and rest for a while," he called to them.

Sarah prepared food and water for the guests. As the men ate they talked. "We'll come back next year," one man said. "By then, Sarah will be the mother of a baby boy." This was amazing news, because Abraham and Sarah were very old—too old to have a baby.

Sarah was listening from inside the tent. When she heard what the man said, it struck her funny to think that she could have a baby. She started laughing and didn't stop until tears were spilling down her wrinkled cheeks.

"Why did Sarah laugh?" the stranger asked Abraham.
"Does she think this is too hard for God?" Abraham was
in shock himself at the news of becoming a father after
all these years. The men left then, but nearly a year
later, Sarah and Abraham were holding their newborn
son, Isaac.

Becoming a Man of God

A man of God believes God.

Abraham and Sarah tried to obey God. They had always wanted a child, but they were both so old now that it seemed impossible. When the man said that Sarah was going to have a baby, Sarah wasn't sure at first, but later she believed him, because when God says he's going to do something, he does it.

A Verse to Remember

We must continue to hold firmly to our declaration of faith. The one who made the promise is faithful.

Hebrews 10:23

No More Teasing

Genesis 21:8–21

Isaac was Sarah's pride and joy. After all, she had waited a long time for this child. When Isaac was still little, Abraham threw a party for him. Everyone ate and played games. Isaac was having a lot of fun—until his step-brother Ishmael began teasing him.

Sarah watched Ishmael's mean game. She heard Isaac's cries, and she became angry. Finally, she stomped across the yard to Abraham. "I want that bully out of here," she demanded.

Abraham told Ishmael's mother, Hagar, that they had to leave. "No, please don't send us away. I won't tease Isaac anymore," Ishmael cried. He didn't want to leave his home. Abraham didn't want him to leave, either. But God told Abraham not to worry because he would take care of Ishmael and Hagar.

Abraham gave Hagar and Ishmael food and water and sent them away. When their food and water were gone Ishmael cried, "I'm thirsty. I want to go home." He became so weak that Hagar was afraid. With tears rolling down her cheeks, she prayed, "God, please take care of my son."

Hagar was crying so hard that she didn't even notice the angel God sent to comfort her. "Hagar," the angel said, "it's all right. God heard Ishmael's cries. He wants you to know that your son will be fine." When Hagar opened her eyes and saw a well, filled to the brim with cool, clear water, she thanked God for his care.

Becoming a Man of God

A man of God knows
God will take care of him.

Hagar was scared. She had no place left to turn, except to God.

God loves his children and loves to take care of them. We can talk to him about whatever we need and he will help us.

What are some ways that God takes care of you?

A Verse to Remember

With perfect peace you will protect those whose minds cannot be changed,
    because they trust you.

Isaiah 26:3

Boys Will Be Boys

Genesis 27:1–28:6

"Esau hit me!" Jacob screamed. Rebekah wondered if her sons would ever stop fighting.

When they grew up Jacob enjoyed helping Rebekah around the house. Esau loved to go hunting with his father.

One afternoon Rebekah heard her husband say, "Esau, I'm old and I can't see very well. You are my oldest son. I want to give you the family blessing. This means you will lead the family after I die. Hunt some wild game and cook my favorite meal. After I eat, I'll give you the blessing."

Jacob should have that blessing, Rebekah thought. "Your father is ready to give the family blessing to your brother. But I'm going to help you get it," she told Jacob.

"We're going to make Father think I'm Esau? Esau has hairy skin, and mine is smooth," Jacob said.

"Put these on your arms so you feel like Esau," Rebekah told Jacob as she put goatskins on him.

When Jacob went to his father, Isaac was confused. "You sound like Jacob but you feel like Esau," he said.

Jacob lied. "I *am* Esau. Give me the blessing, Father."

"May God bless you, may nations serve you, and may you rule over your brothers." It was done. Jacob had stolen Esau's blessing.

When Esau found out, he begged for a blessing from his father too. "You must have a blessing left for me!" But Isaac didn't. Esau was angry. "I'll get even with Jacob!" he vowed.

Later Rebekah told Jacob, "You have to get away until Esau calms down." Jacob left home then.

Becoming a Man of God

A man of God learns from his mistakes.

Jacob and Rebekah knew it was wrong to steal the family blessing. They made a bad choice— we all do that sometimes. But the bad choices they made could not stop God's plan.

Have you ever wanted to get something that you didn't really deserve? What happened?

A Verse to Remember

When he falls, he will not be thrown down headfirst because the Lord holds on to his hand.

Psalm 37:24

One Big Happy Family

Genesis 37–45

"Get me outta here!" Joseph shouted. He tried to climb out of the hole where his brothers had thrown him.

They didn't help him because they were jealous. He was their dad's favorite. Their father even gave Joseph a special colorful coat.

Later some men came by on their way to Egypt. "We can make some money and get rid of Joseph too," one brother said. "Let's sell him to those men." Before Joseph knew it, he was in Egypt—the slave of Potiphar.

Joseph worked hard for Potiphar and was put in charge of the whole household. But one day Potiphar's wife told lies about Joseph and he ended up in jail.

"Hey, Joseph, your prayers work great—look where you are!" The other prisoners made fun of Joseph for his faith in God until the day two of them had strange dreams. God helped Joseph explain what their dreams meant.

Later God helped Joseph explain Pharaoh's dreams too. Pharaoh was so happy that he made Joseph second in command over the whole country.

Then there was a drought in Egypt—no food grew. Joseph had planned ahead and saved up food for the whole country.

One day Joseph's brothers came to buy food. They didn't recognize Joseph, but he knew them. He could have tried to get even with them, but he didn't. Instead he said, "It's me, Joseph. I forgive you for trying to hurt me." That's exactly what God wanted him to do.

Becoming a Man of God

A man of God forgives.

Joseph's brothers were mean to him. But when Joseph had the chance to pay them back, he didn't. He forgave them instead of getting even with them.

Has someone ever done something mean to you? Did you want to get even with them? What do you think God wants you to do?

A Verse to Remember

Even if he wrongs you seven times in one day and comes back to you seven times and says that he is sorry, forgive him.

Luke 17:4

One Determined Momma

Exodus 2:1–10

"I don't care what Pharaoh ordered; no soldiers are taking my baby away!" Jochebed said as she held Moses.

"But Pharaoh gave orders to get rid of all Hebrew baby boys. How do you expect to save our son?" Moses's father wished he had an answer to his own question.

"Miriam, hold the baby. I'll be back soon," Jochebed said. When she came back later, her arms were filled with reeds from the banks of the Nile River. Miriam watched as her mother wove the reeds together into a little basket—just the right size for the baby to fit inside.

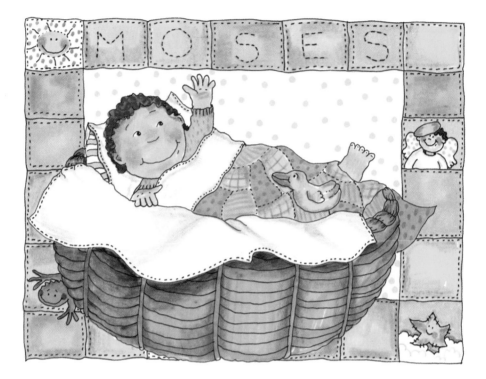

Jochebed hugged baby Moses. Then she laid him in the basket and tucked him in.

Jochebed and Miriam carried the sleeping baby to the Nile River and gently set the basket afloat. "Stay here and watch what happens to him," Jochebed whispered to Miriam.

After her mother went home, Miriam hid behind the reeds on the riverbank. Moses's basket floated close to the place Pharaoh's daughter sometimes came to bathe. *What will happen to Moses if Pharaoh's daughter finds him?* Miriam thought.

A while later Pharaoh's daughter came to the river and saw the floating basket. Miriam could hear her brother crying when the princess looked inside.

The princess wanted to keep the baby, but she needed someone to take care of him. Miriam offered to find someone and ran home. "Momma, the princess found Moses. Hurry—you can take care of him."

Becoming a Man of God

A man of God takes action.

God helped Jochebed come up with a plan to save her son. Sometimes we have to trust God with things. All we can do is wait patiently. But there are also times when God wants us to use our brains. Then we should ask God for wisdom and get busy.

Have you ever been part of a plan for something that needed to be done?

A Verse to Remember

Learn to do good.
Seek justice.
Arrest oppressors.
Defend orphans.
Plead the case of widows.

Isaiah 1:17

Red Sea Panic

Exodus 14

When the Israelites saw the Egyptian army chasing them,
they went straight to Moses.

"We're scared. What's going to happen to us?" they
asked. Moses saw that all the people were afraid.

God had sent ten plagues to get the Israelites out of Egypt, but now the Egyptians were chasing them.

Pharaoh must have realized that without us there was no one to make bricks. So Pharaoh and his whole army have come to bring us back. Now we're trapped with our backs against the Red Sea! Moses thought.

Moses knelt down and prayed. "Are we going to be dragged back to slavery? Dear God, what is going on?"

Of course, God had a plan. God told Moses exactly what to do.

"Be quiet!" Moses called to the frightened people. "Watch what God will do to save you!" He lifted his hand over the sea. Immediately the wind began to blow so hard that the waters blew apart—two big walls of water stood high. It kept blowing until the ground between the walls was completely dry. "Go on through!" Moses ordered.

It took a long time for all the people to cross, even though they hurried as fast as they could.

The Egyptian army raced into the sea, sure that they could catch the Israelites. But when Moses raised his hand over the sea again, the walls of water crashed down, flooding over the soldiers and chariots. God kept every Israelite safe.

Becoming a Man of God

A man of God works for God.

God told Moses just to raise his hand over the sea and when Moses did it the water parted. He was willing to do whatever God told him to do.

Someday God may ask you to do something that you think is too hard. Remember that he won't ask you to do a job without promising to help you do it.

A Verse to Remember

I can do everything through Christ who strengthens me.

Philippians 4:13

And the Walls
Come Tumblin' Down

Joshua 6

After Moses died God chose Joshua to lead his people.

One time the Israelites camped near Jericho, a city surrounded by big walls. God said to Joshua, "I'm giving you this city. Make sure you do what I tell you."

"God said we can capture Jericho," Joshua told the people. We must do exactly what God says: March around the city once a day for six days—without saying a word."

"Who attacks a city by silently marching around it?" the people asked.

"God said it, so we're doing it," Joshua  declared.

Once a day for six days the Israelite army silently marched around the city. By the sixth day, the men of Jericho were making fun of them and the Israelites wondered if Joshua really knew what he was doing.

The seventh day, people in Jericho heard the Israelites marching again. "Why don't they go away?" the people of Jericho said. Some of them noticed that the Israelites didn't stop after one time around. *It's just a new part of their plan*, they thought. Six times Joshua led his people around the city. By then crowds of people were on the walls making fun of the Israelites.

"You're going to wear out your sandals!" people shouted.

As the Israelites started the seventh time around, Joshua yelled, "Shout—the Lord has given you this city!"

So they shouted. The walls crumbled and fell, and the Israelites raced in and captured Jericho. God gave them the city—just as he said.

Becoming a Man of God

A man of God follows instructions.

Joshua was good at following instructions. He believed that God would help the Israelites capture Jericho, but only if they did exactly what he told them to do.

How well do you follow instructions? Are you careful to do exactly what you are told to do?

A Verse to Remember

Love the LORD your God, follow his directions, and keep his commands. Be loyal to him, and serve him with all your heart and soul.

Joshua 22:5

Thank God
for Second Chances

Judges 16

Samson tossed the lion out of his way. Then he flipped his long hair over his shoulder and went on his way. *No one* messed with Samson. He was the strongest man in the world.

Samson was married to a Philistine girl named Delilah. But the Philistines hated Samson and wanted to capture him. They came up with a plan. "Find out where Samson's strength comes from and we'll pay you," they told Delilah. She agreed and asked Samson to tell her the secret of his strength.

Samson teased her by giving her wrong answers like "New ropes will hold me." Delilah tried his suggestions, but each time Samson escaped.

Delilah pouted. "If you loved me you'd tell me the truth."

Finally Samson told her the real secret. "My strength comes from my long hair. If my hair were cut, my strength would be gone."

Delilah waited for Samson to fall asleep, then she called, "Come in, Philistines, and bring your money. Cut off his hair and Samson is yours." Samson woke up while they were tying his arms and tried to flex his muscles, but his strength was gone.

A while later the Philistines paraded Samson around at a party. People made fun of him, but they didn't notice that his hair had grown back.

"God, help me one last time," Samson prayed. Then he pushed on the giant pillars that held up the building. The pillars cracked and the building crashed down, killing Samson and all the Philistines.

Becoming a Man of God

A man of God doesn't let anything come between him and God.

As a young child Samson was dedicated to serve God. He didn't always behave in a way that showed God was important to him. His marriage to a Philistine girl ended up being his downfall, because the Philistines were enemies of God's people.

What things could become too important to you and push God out of first place?

A Verse to Remember

Never have any other god.

Exodus 20:3

Do You Hear Something?

1 Samuel 3

Samuel got in bed and went to sleep. Tomorrow would be busy. He lived in the temple and helped Eli, the priest. Samuel was learning to be a priest himself.

Samuel was sound asleep when he heard, "Samuel, Samuel." He woke up and stumbled into Eli's room.

"Yes, Eli, what do you need?"

"I didn't call you, Samuel; go back to bed," Eli mumbled.

I must have been dreaming, Samuel thought. He went back to bed and fell asleep, but was jolted awake again when he heard, "Samuel, Samuel." He stubbed his toe as he ran to Eli's room.

"I'm here. What do you need?" he said.

"Why did you wake me again? I didn't call you," Eli said, turning his back.

Samuel was confused. He tried to fall asleep but he heard the voice again. "Samuel, Samuel."

Samuel marched into Eli's room.

"Yes, Eli. What do you need?" he asked.

The old priest sat up. Now he knew God was calling Samuel, so he told him what to do.

Samuel went back to bed and waited. Before long he
heard, "Samuel, Samuel."

"Yes, Lord, I'm listening," he answered, just as Eli
had told him to do. "Eli was right; it is God calling me!"
Samuel listened to everything God said. He learned an
important lesson about listening when God calls.

Becoming a Man of God

A man of God listens to God.

Can you imagine hearing God call your name in the middle of the night? God knew that Samuel would pay attention to what he told him.

You may not hear God call your name. But he does speak. What are some ways that God speaks to you?

A Verse to Remember

I will generously pour out my spirit for you.
I will make my words known to you.

Proverbs 1:23

No Fear!

1 Samuel 17

"How can King Saul's soldiers let that giant keep on bullying them?" David wondered.

Twice a day for forty days Goliath shouted, "Send someone out to fight me!" No one volunteered.

Every time David heard the giant he got mad. "How can the soldiers be scared of him? I'm not and I'm just a kid."

David marched into King Saul's tent and announced, "I'll fight the giant!"

King Saul was excited to have a volunteer until he saw the young boy. "What chance do you have against a giant?" he asked. But he had to admit that David looked determined. "At least wear my armor," Saul said.

David put it on, but the armor was so heavy he couldn't move or lift his arms. "I can't even walk in this," David said, and he took it off.

I can still fight the giant, David thought. As he went down the hill toward Goliath, he picked up some rocks and dropped one into his slingshot.

When Goliath saw the boy with the slingshot, he was *angry*! He flexed his muscles and pounded his spear into the ground. David didn't even flinch.

As he got closer to the giant, David swung his sling-shot around his head. Finally, he let go and the rock shot through the air. It hit Goliath right on the forehead. Thud! The giant fell to the ground.

When the Philistine soldiers saw their hero fall, they ran away. The Israelite soldiers shouted and cheered, "David won! God gave him the victory."

Becoming a Man of God

A man of God trusts God's power.

King Saul's soldiers stood around watching as a young boy went to fight the giant that they were all afraid of. Why were none of them able to fight Goliath? Because they didn't believe they had God's power to help them.

Have you ever had to do something that was really hard? Did you ask God to help you?

A Verse to Remember

The LORD is good.
>He is a fortress in the day of trouble.
>He knows those who seek shelter in him.

Nahum 1:7

Loyal Buddies

1 Samuel 20

"Jonathan, why does your dad want to hurt me?" David asked. King Saul had chased him around the countryside and had even thrown spears at him.

"Dad wouldn't hurt you," Jonathan said. "After all, he knows you're my best friend, and he hasn't told me that you have done anything wrong."

"Exactly, he knows we're good friends. That's why he wouldn't tell you. But I'm telling you that I'm in danger!" David responded. "I have a plan—a way we can find out what he's thinking." David explained his idea to Jonathan.

The next day at dinner, King Saul asked, "Where is David?"

"He went to see his family," Jonathan said.

"Go get him so I can get rid of him," King Saul shouted. "As long as he is around, you will never be king!"

Jonathan was sad. Now he knew that his father really did want to hurt David.

Jonathan went out to the field where David was hiding and shot three arrows. Then he sent a servant to get the arrows. "That one arrow is still ahead of you," Jonathan shouted to the servant. That was their signal that meant King Saul wanted to get rid of David. Then David came out and the two friends hugged. They knew that David had to leave and they might never see each other again.

Becoming a Man of God

A man of God is loyal to his friends.

Jonathan and David are examples of true friendship. Jonathan's father wanted to hurt David and that was wrong because David hadn't done anything to deserve that. Jonathan protected David.

Who is your best friend? Have you ever stood up for your friend when someone else was teasing him?

A Verse to Remember

A friend always loves,
   and a brother is born to share trouble.

Proverbs 17:17

The Real God

1 Kings 18:16–40

"Make up your minds," Elijah said to the people. He was tired of them claiming to serve God one day and an idol the next. "If God is God, serve him and forget the others."

Elijah was the only prophet of God, but the idol Baal had 450 prophets. Elijah said, "I challenge the prophets of Baal to a contest. Meet me on Mount Carmel and we'll see who is the real God."

The prophets of Baal built an altar and put a bull on it. Then they danced around and called to Baal, "Send fire down and burn up our offering." Nothing happened.

Finally Elijah said, "Maybe Baal is sleeping." This just made them shout louder.

After listening to them all day Elijah said, "It's my turn."

He built an altar and put a bull on it. He dug a trench around the altar and poured four big jars of water over the whole thing. Then he did it again. And again. Water overflowed the trench. The wood and the bull were soaked.

Elijah stepped back and said, "God, show these people that you are the true God."

Fire shot down from heaven and burned up the bull, the altar, and even the water.

The prophets of Baal were frightened and tried to run away. Meanwhile, the crowd of people who had come to see the contest bowed down to the ground. "The Lord is God!" they shouted.

Becoming a Man of God
A man of God takes a stand.

Elijah believed in God. Even though he was out-numbered, he was sure that God was the real God and that Baal was an idol. He wasn't afraid.

Have you ever taken a stand for God? What happened?

A Verse to Remember

Yet, the strength of those who wait with hope in the LORD will be renewed.
> They will soar on wings like eagles.
>> They will run and won't become weary.
>> They will walk and won't grow tired.

Isaiah 40:31

Fly Away Home

2 Kings 2:1–15

Elisha knew that Elijah would be leaving soon, and he wanted to learn as much as he could from the great prophet of God.

He followed Elijah everywhere. He watched everything Elijah did and hoped to learn from his close walk with God.

One afternoon Elijah and Elisha stopped near the Jordan River. Elisha watched as Elijah carefully folded his robe and slapped it on the waters of the Jordan River. "The waters are parting!" Elisha cried. They crossed through on dry ground.

"What can I do for you before I leave?" Elijah asked.

"I want to be God's prophet like you are," Elisha answered.

"If you see me when I'm taken away you will have what you want." As Elijah finished speaking, a chariot made of fire came between the two men. Elisha was frightened when he saw that Elijah was in the chariot and was flying away!

Elisha stood there for awhile, then he picked up Elijah's robe. He folded it and hit the waters of the Jordan River with it. They divided, just as they had when Elijah hit them. Elisha walked across the river on dry ground and passed a group of prophets from Jericho who had seen everything that happened. As he passed them, they said, "Elisha has taken Elijah's place."

Becoming a Man of God

A man of God
learns from older Christians.

Elisha knew he could learn a lot from Elijah. So he stayed close to him and watched everything he did. When Elijah left, Elisha knew just what to do.

Is there an older person you admire a lot? What do you think you could learn from this person?

A Verse to Remember

Now, sons, listen to me.
> Blessed are those who follow my ways.
> Listen to discipline, and become wise.
> Do not leave my ways.

Proverbs 8:32–33

Olive Oil Overflow

2 Kings 4:1–7

"Momma, do we really have to go live with that man?" the boys asked.

Wasn't it bad enough that the boys' father died? the mother thought. Now this man was saying that her husband owed him lots of money—and if she didn't pay, he would take her sons.

"No, I will not let you go," she said. She hurried to see Elisha. She knew that if anyone could help her, it would be the prophet of God.

"What can I do to help you?" Elisha asked.

"I don't have any money so I can't pay the man what my husband owed. My sons are all I have left. Please don't let him take them," she said.

"What do you have in your house?" Elisha asked.

"Nothing—except one jar of olive oil," she answered.

Elisha said, "Send your sons around to your neighbors' houses. Have them borrow all the empty jars they can find."

The woman sent her sons out right away. When they returned, Elisha told her to take her one jar of olive oil and pour it into one of the empty jars.

She did what he said. "This one is full. Bring another jar," she called to her son. Jar after jar was filled to the brim from the woman's one little jar of oil.

"Now," Elisha said, "sell all that oil and pay the man what you owe him. There will be enough money left over for you to buy food."

Becoming a Man of God

A man of God goes to God for help.

This woman had a problem. She had nothing left but her two sons, and now a man was threatening to take them away. She knew that the best thing to do was ask God's prophet for help.

Have you ever had a problem you didn't know how to solve? Did you talk to God about it?

A Verse to Remember

If any of you needs wisdom to know what you should do, you should ask God, and he will give it to you. God is generous to everyone and doesn't find fault with them.

James 1:5

Veggie Power

Daniel 1

Daniel and his friends were captured by the Babylonians. Because they were young, healthy, and handsome they were put in a special training program to become palace workers.

"You will learn our language. You will learn how to behave in the palace, and, best of all," the prison guard announced, "you won't have to eat prison food. You will be served the king's best food!"

The other young men cheered. But Daniel, Shadrach, Meshach, and Abednego weren't so happy.

"That food is offered to idols before it's served to us," Daniel told his friends. "We can't eat it because it would not be honoring God." The friends came up with a plan.

"Sir," Daniel said to the guard, "my friends and I want vegetables and water instead of the king's food."

"If you aren't as strong as the other young men the king will be angry," the guard said.

"Well, how about a test?" Daniel asked. "Give us vegetables and water for ten days; if we don't look as good as everyone else by that time we will eat the king's food." The guard agreed to let them try it.

After ten days, Daniel and his friends were stronger and healthier than all the other boys.

God blessed Daniel, Shadrach, Meshach, and Abednego because they honored him. At the end of the training the king was more impressed with these four boys than any of the others.

Becoming a Man of God

A man of God refuses to compromise.

It was very brave of Daniel to ask for special permission to eat different food than the other prisoners. The friends' witness for God was very important to them, and they weren't willing to compromise.

In what way can you show how important your witness for God is?

A Verse to Remember

Love the Lord your God with all your heart, with all your soul, and with all your mind.

Matthew 22:37

Out of the Frying Pan and into the Fire

Daniel 3

King Nebuchadnezzar thought he was important and he wanted everyone to know it. "This giant statue of me is awesome. I want to be sure everyone notices it." The king ordered that anytime people heard music, they should bow down and worship the statue.

"There is no way I am worshiping that statue," Shadrach declared. Meshach and Abednego agreed. The three friends loved God. They knew it would be wrong to worship anything besides him.

"These boys refuse to bow to your statue," a guard reported to the king.

"Is this true?" the king's voice boomed.

Shadrach took a deep breath. "Yes, sir, we serve God and we will worship only him."

"Throw these men into the fire," the king ordered. Shadrach, Meshach, and Abednego were not afraid. "We trust our God to take care of us," they said.

A guard pushed the three boys into the blazing hot furnace. When Shadrach looked over at his friends, he noticed the flames weren't harming them. "It's hot, but we're not burning up," he exclaimed.

"How many guys did you throw in there?" the young men heard the king asking his guards.

"Three, your highness."

"Well, then, who is that fourth man? He looks like an angel. Get them out here!" King Nebuchadnezzar roared.

Shadrach, Meshach, and Abednego weren't burned at all. The angel had protected them. "I told you our God would take care of us," Shadrach said.

"I see what you mean," the king had to admit. "Your God rescued you."

Becoming a Man of God

*A man of God believes
in God's protection.*

It's easy to trust in God's protection when everything is going fine, but it's harder in a scary situation. The three boys in the story believed God would rescue them.

The foundation of trust in God is like a tower that has a new layer added every day. What are the ways you see God's care and protection every single day?

A Verse to Remember

Because you love me, I will rescue you.
  I will protect you because you know my name.

Psalm 91:14

Here Kitty, Kitty

Daniel 6

"We have to get rid of Daniel. King Darius wants to make him our boss. And he's just a slave," the officials said.

The men looked for ways to get Daniel in trouble. But they couldn't find anything. Then one said, "I have a plan."

The plan was to trick the king into signing a law that people couldn't pray to anyone except the king.

Daniel heard about the new law but kept right on praying to God. He knelt in front of his bedroom window and prayed. Little did Daniel know that his enemies were watching him.

The officials couldn't wait to tell the king. "Daniel prayed. We saw him. Throw him to the lions. It's the law and you can't change it."

King Darius sent for Daniel. "I've been tricked," he said. "I'm so sorry, Daniel, but I have to obey the law."

"God will take care of me," Daniel said. The guards threw him into a pit full of hungry lions, then slid a big stone over the top. There was no way out.

The king paced around his room worrying about Daniel. *I know when the stone is moved tomorrow we'll find that the lions have eaten Daniel,* he thought.

He didn't know God protected Daniel by sending angels to keep the lions' mouths shut.

In the morning King Darius
rushed to the lions' den. "Daniel,
did your God protect you?" he
called.

"Yes," Daniel called back. "I haven't done anything wrong toward God or you. So he kept the lions'
mouths shut."

"Daniel's God is the real God," King Darius said.
"Everyone should worship him."

Becoming a Man of God

*A man of God knows God will
do the right thing.*

Daniel knew he hadn't done anything wrong. He obeyed and honored God. Daniel didn't hide his prayer because he knew that God knew his heart and that he could trust him no matter what. Is it sometimes hard for you to do the right thing?

A Verse to Remember

God is our refuge and strength,
an ever-present help in times of trouble.

Psalm 46:1

The Fish That Didn't Get Away

Jonah 1–4

Jonah was furious when God told him to go to Nineveh. "I won't go! I don't like those people, and if I tell them about you, they might repent of their sins and then you'll forgive them." Then Jonah tried to run away from God.

At the first ship he saw, Jonah asked, "Where is this boat going?"

"Tarshish," the sailor said.

"Great. That's in the opposite direction of Nineveh," Jonah said. He went straight to the belly of the ship and lay down to sleep. *Not even God can find me here,* he thought as the rocking of the ship lulled him to sleep.

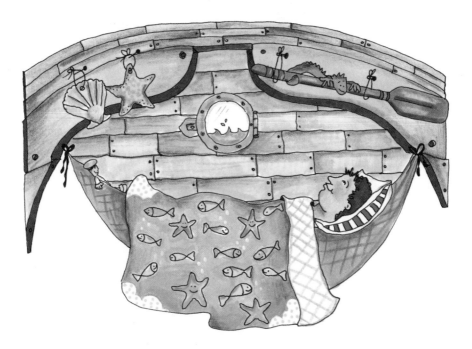

Meanwhile, the sailors had a problem. One of them called out, "I've never seen a storm blow like this. We're going to sink. Throw boxes overboard. Lower the sails. Hurry!"

Jonah slept through the whole thing until a sailor shouted, "If you have a god, pray to him because we're in big trouble!"

"Look, this storm is all my fault—I was hiding from God," Jonah told the sailors. "Toss me overboard and the storm will stop."

The sailors didn't want to hurt Jonah, but they wanted to save their boat so they threw Jonah overboard.

He had barely hit the water when a huge fish swallowed him. For three days and nights Jonah was in the belly of the great fish.

He had time to think about how he had disobeyed God. He felt bad. "I'm sorry, God," he said. "I should have obeyed you. If you still want me to go to Nineveh, I'll go." The big fish spit Jonah onto the beach and he immediately went to Nineveh.

Becoming a Man of God

A man of God obeys immediately.

Jonah should have obeyed God the first time. But God gave him a second chance and then Jonah went to Nineveh.

When was a time that you didn't obey and were punished? What was the punishment?

A Verse to Remember

If you obey my commandments, you will live in my love. I have obeyed my Father's commandments, and in that way I live in his love.

John 15:10

Read My Lips

Luke 1:5–25, 57–64

Zechariah was serving in the temple when an angel appeared to him and said, "You and Elizabeth will have a baby." Zechariah refused to believe it—he and his wife were very old. "Since you do not believe God's message you will not be able to speak until the baby is born," the angel said. Zechariah rushed home to see his wife.

Elizabeth had never seen her husband so excited but he was not able to speak. "You have something to tell me, right? Just say it." But he couldn't. Finally, he grabbed a broom and wrote in the dirt, "We're going to have a baby."

"Do you think a baby could grow in this old body?" Elizabeth grabbed her broom and started back to the house. But then she stopped. "You're serious, aren't you?" Suddenly her knees felt weak. *A baby*, she thought. *After all these years I'm going to have a baby!*

The next few months were spent getting things ready for the baby's birth. Zechariah wished he could tell his wife how excited he was about having a child who would tell the world that the Messiah was coming.

When their son was born, Zechariah and Elizabeth's relatives came to help them celebrate. Everyone had an opinion of what the baby's name should be. Zechariah took a tablet and wrote **His name is John;** then he held it up for all to see. (That's what the angel had told Zechariah to name him.) Zechariah's voice came back, and he and Elizabeth praised God.

Becoming a Man of God

A man of God is sometimes quiet.

Zechariah was alone in the temple doing his work as a priest, so it was probably quiet. When he didn't believe the angel's message and God took his voice away it was definitely quiet.

It's very hard to hear God speak, or anyone else for that matter, if you are always making noise.

A Verse to Remember

Let go of your concerns!
    Then you will know that I am God.

    Psalm 46:10

A Trusting Stepdad

Matthew 1:20–25; Luke 2:1–20

"Joseph, God knows you are confused. Mary was telling you the truth. The baby she's going to have is the Son of God." Joseph didn't usually dream about angels— and yet here was one in his dream and it was speaking to him.

Joseph took Mary with him to Bethlehem.

"Are you okay, Mary?" Joseph felt bad that Mary was taking this long trip on a donkey. "We'll be there soon. Then we'll find a place to stay and you can rest," Joseph promised.

"I don't feel very good," Mary said as they arrived in Bethlehem.

"I'll go in this inn and get a room," Joseph said. In a few minutes he was back. "It's full. There aren't any rooms left in all of Bethlehem. The best we can get is a spot in the stable."

Joseph made a bed for Mary to lie on. She fell asleep right away. Sometime later she shook Joseph awake and said, "The baby is coming!" The animals were very quiet when Joseph placed the baby boy in Mary's arms.

In the early light of dawn Joseph looked up to see shepherds peeking over the stable door. "An angel told us that your baby is the Messiah. We came to worship him." Mary wasn't surprised by what they said. Joseph remembered the words of the angel in his dream: "This child will save his people from their sins."

It's true, he thought. *The angel's words were true.*

Becoming a Man of God

A man of God trusts God's plan.

Joseph and Mary had been planning their wedding for quite a while. But God had other plans. The news that Mary was expecting a baby was definitely not in their plans. Joseph trusted God and continued with the wedding.

How can you trust God's plan?

A Verse to Remember

Trust the LORD with all your heart,
   and do not rely on your own understanding.

Proverbs 3:5

Night Flight

Matthew 2:1-23

Sometimes Joseph nearly forgot that Jesus wasn't a boy like every other boy. But Joseph was reminded when wise men from another country brought gifts to Jesus and worshiped him.

A few days after the wise men left, an angel visited Joseph in a dream again. "Get your family out of town. King Herod wants to kill Jesus." Joseph was worried. *God is trusting us to raise his Son*, he thought. *I can't let Herod hurt him.*

HURRY UP!

"Mary, get up. Dress the baby. We have to leave town now," Joseph said. "Jesus's life is in danger." Joseph and his family left that night.

Joseph, Mary, and Jesus settled in Egypt. *I wonder how long we'll be here*, Mary thought. Finally, one night the angel came back to Joseph in another dream. "King Herod is dead," the angel said. "It is safe to take Jesus home now."

Joseph and Mary were so happy to be able to go home.
Instead of returning to Bethlehem, the little family went
home to Nazareth.

Becoming a Man of God

A man of God protects.

Joseph knew that he should follow the instructions the angel gave him because the most important thing was to protect Jesus from King Herod.

When has your mom or dad protected you? It's a nice feeling to know that someone is keeping you safe, isn't it?

A Verse to Remember

The LORD guards you as you come and go,
    now and forever.

Psalm 121:8

A Child Shall Lead Them

Luke 2:41–52

"I love going to Jerusalem for the Passover Festival. May I walk with my friends?" Jesus asked.

"I think you're old enough to walk with your friends this year," Mary said. "But let's eat dinner now. We still have a lot to do before we leave tomorrow morning."

Early the next morning Jesus was dressed and waiting at the door when his parents got up. Soon they were in the middle of the crowd walking to Jerusalem. "Jesus, over here!" someone called. He ran to join his friends. The Passover celebration was wonderful. It was a time to thank God for taking care of his people.

When the festival ended, everyone headed home. "Have you seen Jesus?" Mary asked.

"No, he's probably with his friends," Joseph answered.

A while later one of Jesus's friends came up. "Where's Jesus?" he asked.

"We thought he was with you," Mary answered.

"No, we haven't seen him all day," the boy said.

Mary grabbed Joseph's hand and they ran back to Jerusalem to look for Jesus. "He's only twelve. What will happen to him? How could we have left him behind?" Mary said.

For three days Mary and Joseph searched the city, up and down the streets, everywhere they could think to look. Jesus was nowhere to be found.

They heard someone mention a boy who was talking to the temple teachers about God. Mary and Joseph ran to the temple. It was Jesus! "We've looked everywhere for you," Mary told him.

Jesus said, "Didn't you know that I would be in my Father's house?" Then he went home with Mary and Joseph

Becoming a Man of God

A man of God never gives up.

Imagine the panic Mary and Joseph must have felt. God trusted them to take care of his Son and they lost him. Immediately Mary and Joseph began searching for Jesus. For three days they looked everywhere for him. Mary and Joseph didn't give up—they kept looking until they found Jesus.

A Verse to Remember

With faith and love for Christ Jesus, consider what you heard me say to be the pattern of accurate teachings.

2 Timothy 1:13

Go Fish!

Luke 5:1-11

"Would you mind pushing the boat out from shore a bit?" Jesus asked.

Peter didn't know who Jesus was, but he pushed the boat out a little farther. Peter cleaned his nets while he listened to Jesus teach the crowd of people on shore.

When Jesus finished teaching, Peter expected him to leave. But instead Jesus said, "Go out there where the water is deeper and let your nets down. You will catch lots of fish."

"Teacher, my partners and I worked hard all night and we didn't catch a single fish. But if you say so, I'll lower the nets."

Peter dropped his fishing net into the water. It instantly filled with so many fish that he couldn't pull it up. "What is going on?" he asked his partners. "The net is ripping!" They filled two boats with all the fish they caught.

Peter looked over at Jesus, who had a smile on his face. Then Peter knew that this man was holy.

Peter dropped to his knees. "Don't be afraid," Jesus said. "From now on you will fish for people." Peter and his partners left their fishing boats on the shore and went with him.

Becoming a Man of God

A man of God follows Jesus.

Jesus has different jobs for each of us to do. Peter was a fisherman before he met Jesus, so Jesus explained that Peter's work would now be to fish for men. In other words, Peter would tell people about Jesus and his love.

What job might Jesus have for you?

A Verse to Remember

Come, follow me! I will teach you how to catch people instead of fish.

Matthew 4:19

Storm Warning

Luke 8:22-25

"I'm tired. How does Jesus keep going?" Peter said.

"You know Jesus—as long as there are people who want to hear about God, he will keep teaching," John said.

Jesus had been teaching for hours, and the disciples were listening to him.

"Looks like he's about finished," Peter said. "Let's get going." But instead of going to the nearby town, Jesus wanted to cross the lake.

"I was hoping we could go to town and get some dinner," one disciple said.

"It's best to do what Jesus says," Peter said. So the disciples climbed into the boat, and Jesus went to sleep in the back.

About halfway across the lake the wind started toss-
ing the little boat around.

"Lower the sail!" someone shouted. "Where is Jesus?"

Someone ran to the back and woke up Jesus. "Don't you care that we're going to drown?"

Jesus stood up and looked at the waves. "Be quiet!" he ordered. Instantly the sea was calm again. The wind stopped, the rain stopped, and the waves were gentle.

"What just happened?"

"How did he do that?"

Jesus looked at his friends. "Where is your faith?" he asked.

Jesus lay down again, but the disciples kept asking each other, "Who is he? Even the wind and waves do what he tells them to do."

Becoming a Man of God

*A man of God believes Jesus
can do anything.*

The disciples were scared of the storm because they didn't understand that Jesus is more powerful than any storm—or anything else.

What kinds of things scare you? Do you talk to God about them?

A Verse to Remember

The LORD rules as king.
    Let the earth rejoice.
    Let all the islands be joyful.

Psalm 97:1

Bread and Fish
for Everyone

John 6:1–13

"Mom, Jesus is in town. May I go?" the little boy cried.

"I guess so, but let me make a lunch for you."

"I don't need a lunch," the boy said, edging toward the door.

"Don't worry. It won't take long."

Soon the boy was headed to town.

There are thousands of people here, the boy thought.
He found a spot close to the front and sat down. Jesus
talked for a long time about God's love. Pretty soon
one of Jesus's helpers said, "It's late, Master. Send the
people home for dinner."

But Jesus said, "No. You give them dinner."

"We don't have any food or money," the man argued.

"Sir, you can have my lunch," the little boy said, holding up his small bundle.

Jesus's helper said, "That little lunch won't do any good with all these people to feed."

But Jesus smiled at the boy as he took the lunch and prayed, "Thank you, God, for this food."

Then he broke the bread and fish into pieces and the disciples passed it out to the people. They kept coming back and Jesus kept giving them more and more. "How did he do that?" the boy said to himself.

Jesus's helpers walked through the crowd, picking up leftover food. "There must be five thousand people here," one disciple said. "Everyone ate all they wanted and there are twelve baskets of leftovers." The boy saw Jesus smiling at him. *Wow!* he thought. *I shared my lunch and helped with a miracle!*

Becoming a Man of God

A man of God shares.

When the little boy heard that Jesus needed food for the people, he gave his whole lunch. He didn't take out some for himself—he shared it all. What can you share with Jesus?

A Verse to Remember

Always do for other people everything you want them to do for you. That is the meaning of Moses' Teachings and the Prophets.

Matthew 7:12

Ghost Man Walking?

Matthew 14:22–33

"Hey, do you see something out there on the water?" one of the disciples asked.

"Yeah, what do you think it is? There's someone or something out there. Even in this storm I can see it." The disciples leaned out over the water, trying to see what it was.

"I wish Jesus was here," John said "I always feel better when he's with us."

"Me too. This storm is getting pretty bad. I hope our boat doesn't take on much more water."

"That ghost is getting closer, and the wind is blowing harder."

"Dear God, please protect us," Peter prayed, squeezing his eyes shut.

"Don't be afraid. It's me." Peter opened one eye and saw Jesus walking on top of the stormy water.

"Jesus, if it's really you, let me walk to you on the water!" Peter shouted.

"Come to me," Jesus called.

Peter walked on top of the water too. Suddenly he realized how strong the wind was and became afraid. Then he began to sink. "Help—save me!"

Jesus pulled him up and said, "You don't have much faith, do you? Didn't you believe I could keep you safe?"

The other disciples helped Peter and Jesus climb into the boat. When they were safely inside, the wind stopped blowing. The men dropped to their knees in worship. "This man really is the Son of God," one of them whispered.

Becoming a Man of God

A man of God keeps his eyes on Jesus.

Peter did fine as long as he kept his eyes on Jesus. But the minute he started looking around at the waves and the storm, he began to sink—he took his eyes off Jesus, the one who could keep him safe.

How good are you at keeping your eyes on what you're doing, no matter what else is going on?

A Verse to Remember

Praise the LORD, my soul,
    and never forget all the good he has done.

Psalm 103:2

Little Man, Big Change

Luke 19:1–10

"Get out of my way; I want to see Jesus too!" Zacchaeus shouted; but no one let the little man through.

Tax collectors like Zacchaeus were not popular because they cheated people out of their money.

"There's Jesus." The words rolled through the crowd and people pushed closer to the road. Zacchaeus had an idea. He scooted up a tree and out to the edge of a branch in time to see people come down the road. *That man in the middle must be Jesus*, thought Zacchaeus.

Finally, the crowd passed below where Zacchaeus sat. He nearly fell off the branch when Jesus looked up and said, "Zacchaeus, come down. I want to stay at your house today."

He knows my name, Zacchaeus thought. He jumped down and led the way to his house.

Zacchaeus wanted to be sure everyone knew that Jesus was coming to his house.

"Why is Jesus going with that cheater?" people complained. "He doesn't deserve to have Jesus spend time with him." Zacchaeus ignored every comment and invited Jesus into his home.

As Jesus and Zacchaeus talked, the tax collector understood how wrong it was for him to cheat. "I promise to change. I will pay back the people I cheated. In fact, I'll pay back four times more than I owe."

Jesus smiled at Zacchaeus. He knew that Zacchaeus loved God now and would treat people honestly.

Becoming a Man of God

*A man of God changes
when he meets Jesus.*

Zacchaeus was a cheater who didn't have any
friends. Until he met Jesus. Then Zacchaeus saw
that he was sinning and he wanted to change. He
wanted to live the way Jesus wanted him to live.

A Verse to Remember

God loved the world this way: He gave his only Son
so that everyone who believes in him will not die but
will have eternal life.

John 3:16

Dad Always Liked You Best

Luke 15:11–32

"I'm tired of working on this farm. I want more excitement," the young man whined.

"Quit complaining and get busy," his older brother said. He was tired of his brother's whining.

"You can stay on this farm, but I want to leave."

The younger son went to his father. "I want my inheritance now. Then I can move to the city."

His father gave him the money and watched him leave. The young man started spending money—restaurants, parties, gifts for his friends. In no time the money was gone.

"The only job I can find is feeding pigs. Even the pigs have food to eat, but I don't. I would be better off going back to my father and begging forgiveness," the young man said. He left the city and headed home.

When he was close to home, his father ran to meet him. "I've been waiting for you!"

The father told his servants to cook a fancy meal and put a purple robe and gold ring on his son. "My son is home and we're going to celebrate."

When the older son heard about the party he said, "I've been doing my work *and* my brother's. No one threw a party for me, even though I've been the good son all this time."

His father said, "Don't you understand? I thought your brother was gone forever, but now he is home. I have to celebrate!"

Jesus told this story to show an example of how God forgives us for doing wrong things and welcomes us back to him.

Becoming a Man of God

A man of God receives forgiveness.

The young man in this story learned a lesson. He was sorry for the way he treated his father and he wanted to come home. But he thought what he had done was so terrible that his father could never forgive him. He was wrong. His father loved him—no matter what—and he forgave him. God wants to forgive you for any bad things you do too. He loves you.

A Verse to Remember

God is faithful and reliable. If we confess our sins, he forgives them and cleanses us from everything we've done wrong.

1 John 1:9

A Friend in Need
Is a Friend Indeed

Luke 10:30–37

What a nice day for my walk to Jericho, the man thought. Just then a couple of thieves jumped out from behind a rock and knocked him down. "Let me up!" he screamed. But one of the robbers hit him and left him bleeding on the side of the road. When the man woke up, his money was gone.

When he heard footsteps, he struggled to lift his head. *It's a priest. If anyone will help me he will,* he thought.

But the priest looked at him with disgust. Then he crossed the road and kept right on walking.

The hurt man heard footsteps again. It was a temple worker. The poor man called weakly, "Please help me." The temple worker came up to the man. *This fellow has been beaten up,* he thought, *but I'm too busy to help.* He stepped over the man and kept right on walking.

It was nearly dark before the man heard more footsteps. This time he didn't even open his eyes until he felt a gentle hand lift his head. *A Samaritan. Why would he stop to help me?* the man thought.

When he woke he was lying in a soft bed. The Samaritan had put bandages on his wounds. He saw the good Samaritan give the innkeeper gold pieces to take care of him. He knew he didn't have anything to worry about now.

Becoming a Man of God

A man of God doesn't have favorites.

The priest and the temple worker in this story did not help the man who was hurt even though they all lived in the same area. Sometimes people who need our help—or who help us—may be different from us.

Do you know any people whose skin is a different color from yours, or people who speak a different language than you?

A Verse to Remember

I'm giving you a new commandment: Love each other in the same way that I have loved you.

John 13:34

A Heartbroken Mom

Luke 7:11–17

"Momma, I don't feel good," the little boy said, crawling up on his mom's lap.

The loving mother did everything she could think of but her little boy got sicker. "Dear God, my son is all I have left," she prayed.

Even with her constant attention, the little boy died. Friends came over with food and flowers. Some of them started making funeral arrangements.

On the day of the funeral a crowd of family and friends
followed along. As they walked through town, people
on the streets stopped and looked, feeling bad for the
sad mother.

At the city gate a group of men stepped aside to let the funeral pass. The men said, "It's not hard to see who the mother of the dead boy is. Tears are falling on her feet." Suddenly one man stepped out of the crowd and took the woman's hand. "Don't be sad," he said. How could the woman not be sad that her son was dead?

But they all knew that the man was Jesus when he took the dead boy's hand and said, "Get up!" To everyone's amazement, the boy sat up. Jesus still held the woman's hand in his, and he gently pressed her son's hand into it. The woman thanked Jesus for bringing her son back to life.

Becoming a Man of God

*A man of God thanks God
for all he does.*

Imagine how excited that mother must have been. The thing she wanted so much was done for her! She probably couldn't say thank you enough times. What would you like to thank God for?

A Verse to Remember

Give thanks to the LORD.
Call on his name.
Make known among the nations what he has done.

1 Chronicles 16:8

Spring Cleaning

Matthew 21:12-17

"Doves for sale. Get your sacrificial birds here!" Loud voices rang through the temple. Signs saying "Change your money to temple coins here" hung from the columns.

Jesus pushed his way through the crowds. "People come here to worship God, but the temple is so noisy, how can anyone even think of God? And these men selling doves and changing money—they are trying to get rich!"

With every step Jesus took he felt more frustrated. "This is not the way to treat God's house," he said. Walking up to a moneychanger's table, Jesus swiped his arm across it and coins went flying. Then he started turning tables upside down.

"This is God's house—my Father's house—and it is meant to be a place of prayer. It is not a place for you to make money by cheating people who come to worship God." Jesus worked his way up the aisle, turning over tables, scattering doves, and spilling money.

The merchants ran, afraid of what Jesus would do next. But he was finished. Then people surrounded him in the courtyard, begging for healing. Children climbed into his lap. Shouts of "Praise God for the Son of David!" echoed through the temple.

Becoming a Man of God

A man of God respects God's house.

Jesus felt very strongly that God's house was a special place for worship. He wanted it to be treated with respect.

What is your church like? Are you quiet and respectful when you go in?

A Verse to Remember

I was glad when they said to me,
"Let's go to the house of the LORD."

Psalm 122:1

Through the Roof

Mark 2:3-12

The man couldn't walk so he lay in bed all day. The highlight of his day was when his friends came to visit.

Four of the man's friends often stopped to talk. One night as the friends started home they asked each other, "Isn't there something we could do to help him?" Soon they came up with a plan.

The next day they lifted their paralyzed friend onto a cot. "Where are we going?" the man asked. His friends just told him to enjoy the ride. They carried him to a little house crowded with people who were listening to Jesus teach.

"Coming through!" the men shouted, trying to get their friend to Jesus. But instead of moving aside, the crowd moved closer together.

Well, that's that, thought the man. *At least they tried. I know Jesus could heal me, but not if they can't get me to him.* However, the four friends didn't give up so easily.

The men grabbed the cot and carried it up to the rooftop. They dug at the grass and tiles on the roof until there was a hole big enough to lower the cot into the room—right in front of Jesus.

Jesus looked up at the four friends peering through the hole in the roof. When he saw their faith in him, he said to the paralyzed man, "Get up and walk." And he did!

Becoming a Man of God

A man of God is part of a team.

The four friends didn't give up. They worked together and got their friend to Jesus. Just one of the friends may not have been able to help—it took all four of them working together.

Have you ever been on a team? What kind? Was it fun?

A Verse to Remember

You are Christ's body and each of you is an individual part of it.

1 Corinthians 12:27

Devoted Sisters

John 11:1-44

"Mary, it's your turn," Martha whispered. The sisters were taking turns sitting with their sick brother, Lazarus.

Lazarus had been sick for several days, and no matter what the sisters did, he did not get better.

One afternoon Mary heard that Jesus was in a nearby town. Mary ran home to tell Martha. "I know Jesus can help Lazarus," she said. The sisters sent a message to him: "Lazarus is very sick. Please come quickly!"

One day passed, then two. Mary and Martha waited for Jesus to come. Meanwhile, Lazarus got worse. Then one night he died.

"Why didn't Jesus come?" Mary asked through her tears. Martha shook her head. She too wondered why Jesus hadn't come; she was disappointed.

A few days later a friend ran into the house and said, "Jesus is coming."

"Now he comes—when Lazarus is already buried. Where was Jesus when he could have helped my brother?" When Martha went to meet Jesus, her frustration spilled out. "If you had been here, Lazarus wouldn't have died!" she said.

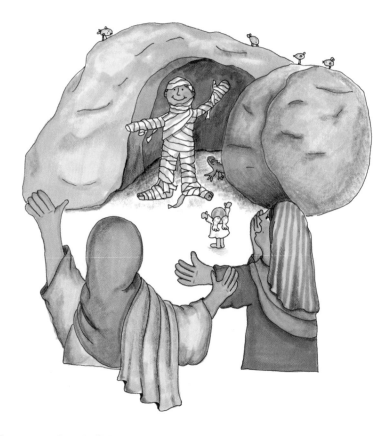

Jesus asked, "Where is Lazarus buried?" They led him to the tomb, wondering what he was going to do. "Open the tomb," Jesus commanded.

Jesus waited while the stone was moved then he called, "Lazarus, come out!" Mary closed her eyes and hid behind Martha. When she looked up she saw Lazarus standing in the tomb door—alive and well!

Becoming a Man of God

A man of God tells God how he feels.

Mary and Martha told Jesus how they felt. They knew that Jesus could take it. Jesus knows our hearts, so we might as well tell him how we feel. We can tell him when we're disappointed or hurt. He won't stop loving us.

Have you ever been disappointed or sad about how God answered a prayer or handled a situation? Did you tell him?

A Verse to Remember

The LORD is near to everyone who prays to him,
to every faithful person who prays to him.

Psalm 145:18

A Dark Day in History

John 19:16–30

Mary held a friend's arm to steady herself.

A Roman soldier snapped a whip across Jesus's back. "Get moving!" he ordered. Jesus dragged the wooden cross slowly down the road.

Mary's heart ached as the crowds of people shouted at her son, "Look at the king of the Jews now!" She looked away. It was too heartbreaking to see what they were doing to Jesus.

At the hill called Calvary the soldiers threw Jesus to the ground and nailed his hands and feet to the wooden cross. When they dropped the cross into the ground, Mary pushed her way to the front, standing right below Jesus.

Jesus was kind and loving and had never done anything wrong. Mary remembered when the angel told her that she was going to have a baby and that he would be the Messiah—the one who would save his people. *This must be what the angel meant,* she thought.

Mary looked into Jesus's eyes—the eyes of her son—the eyes of God's Son. Despite all the terrible things happening to him his eyes were filled with love, even for the people killing him.

Then Jesus said, "It is finished." When he died, Mary was sad, but she knew that Jesus had come to earth to save everyone who believes in him.

Becoming a Man of God

*A man of God understands
Jesus died on the cross for him.*

A loving mom would do almost anything to help
her son. But there wasn't anything Mary could
do about her son dying. This was why Jesus
came to earth. He was willing to go through all
of this because he loves us so much.

A Verse to Remember

Clearly, Christ's love guides us. We are convinced of
the fact that one man has died for all people. There-
fore, all people have died.

2 Corinthians 5:14

The Empty Tomb

Mark 16:1–7

The sun was just peeking over the horizon when three women began to walk to the cemetery. They were sad that Jesus died. Jesus taught them so much about God, but then he died—could they believe anything he said?

Even in the middle of their sadness the women wanted to do the right thing—that's what they had been taught their whole lives. So they were going to anoint Jesus's body with oil and perfumes.

The women had known each other for years, but today none of them knew what to say. Then one of them remembered the big stone. Several soldiers had pushed it in front of the tomb. "How are we going to move that stone?" the woman wondered.

"Come on, we'll figure something out," one of the friends said. As they came near the tomb, the woman in front suddenly stopped.

"It's gone," she whispered. "The stone is gone, and the tomb is open." The women looked at each other. What could this mean?

The bravest of the three women stumbled into the open tomb. She fell to her knees when a voice said, "I know you're looking for Jesus. He's not here. He is alive. He came back to life just as he said he would."

"He's alive!" the woman shouted to her friends. "Praise God; Jesus is alive!"

Becoming a Man of God

*A man of God knows God will do
what he says.*

The poor women going to the tomb were sad because they had forgotten what Jesus said he would do. Jesus said he would come back to life, but they didn't believe him. Do you believe Jesus?

A Verse to Remember

You're looking for Jesus from Nazareth, who was crucified. He has been brought back to life. He's not here. Look at the place where they laid him.

Mark 16:6

No Leg to Stand On

Acts 3:1–10

Every day the man's friends carried him to the same place near the Beautiful Gate of Jerusalem. Crowds of people poured in and out of the city every day. He had a good spot for begging.

Day in and day out the man begged for money. He was unable to walk so he couldn't get a job.

This day started out like any other. First the trip to the Gate, then his constant begging. When he saw Peter and John walk by he said, "Please, can you spare some change for a crippled old man?"

He waited for them to give him money. Instead they said, "We don't have any money for you."

"Then move out of the way," the beggar said.

"I have something better than money," one of the men said. The old man couldn't imagine anything better than money, but he was interested. So he waited. Then the man said, "In the name of Jesus of Nazareth, get up and walk!"

The crippled man felt a strange tingling in his legs and feet. He had never felt *anything* in his legs and feet. Dead muscles zoomed to life, crooked bones straightened. Peter took the man's arms and lifted him to his feet. Joy flooded through his body. "Praise God!" he shouted as he ran and jumped.

Becoming a Man of God

A man of God desires God's best.

The beggar in this story wanted money. That's as far as his dream went. He didn't dare hope for anything better. He almost missed receiving God's wonderful gift of healing because he wasn't thinking that big. What would you like God to do for you?

A Verse to Remember

The payment for sin is death, but the gift that God freely gives is everlasting life found in Christ Jesus our Lord.

Romans 6:23

One Hundred Yard Dash

Acts 8:26-40

"Philip, go down the road that goes from Jerusalem to Gaza," the angel of God said. Philip started walking toward Gaza, even though he didn't know why he was going there.

After a while a fancy carriage came down the road. As it passed, Philip saw a man from Ethiopia inside. *He must be important in the government to be in such a nice carriage,* Philip thought. The Holy Spirit told Philip to run along beside it. When Philip got closer, he heard the man inside reading from the book of Isaiah.

"Do you understand what you're reading?" Philip called to the man.

"No," he answered. "How can I understand it unless someone explains it. Do you understand it?"

"Yes. I can tell you what it means." So the man stopped his carriage and Philip climbed in.

"These verses are talking about Jesus of Nazareth," Philip explained. He also read other verses about why Jesus came to earth. Philip told the Ethiopian the whole story of God's wonderful love.

"Stop the carriage," the man ordered. "Look, there is some water over there. Why can't I be baptized right now? I believe what you are telling me about Jesus."

So Philip baptized him. The Ethiopian praised God for the good news about Jesus.

Becoming a Man of God

*A man of God shares God's love
with others.*

Philip had information that would help the man
in the chariot understand God's Word. He was
willing to share that good news even though he
had to change his plans to talk to the man.

Have you shared God's Word with anyone?

A Verse to Remember

Your word is a lamp for my feet
 and a light for my path.

Psalm 119:105

A Changed Heart

Acts 9:1–19

Every time Saul thought about Christians he became angry. *I'm getting rid of all Christians if it's the last thing I do*, he thought.

After years of throwing the Christians in Jerusalem in jail, Saul said, "My work here is done. I'll go to Damascus and get rid of the Christians there." He and his friends began the walk to Damascus. Then Saul heard a voice say, "Saul, why are you persecuting me?" He looked around but didn't see anyone.

"Saul, why are you persecuting me?" This time a blinding light shined on Saul. He crawled on his hands and knees trying to get away from it. But the light moved with him and the voice kept asking, "Saul, why are you persecuting me?"

Saul's friends couldn't figure out where the voice was coming from.

"Who are you?" Saul asked.

"I am Jesus, the one you are persecuting."

Saul hung his head. *It's true then*, he thought. *Jesus is real. The Christians have been right all along. I'm the one who has been wrong.* Right there on the road to Damascus Saul asked for forgiveness for everything he had done.

Saul's heart was changed. He no longer wanted to hurt Christians; now he was a Christian too. God changed Saul's name to Paul. Saul's life had been devoted to getting rid of Christians—Paul's life was devoted to winning people to Christ.

Becoming a Man of God

*A man of God gives
his whole life to God.*

Paul (Saul) was a pretty bad guy before he believed in Jesus. He tried to hurt Christians. But after he believed in Jesus, Paul devoted his whole life to telling others about God.

Do you think about living for God or sharing his love with others every day?

A Verse to Remember

Come close to God, and he will come close to you. Clean up your lives, you sinners, and clear your minds, you doubters.

James 4:8

A Special Escort

Acts 12:1–17

I'm so tired, Peter thought. *It's hard to sleep when I am chained to two guards.* They finally settled down on the floor of the prison cell to try to get some rest.

I'm only in prison because I teach about Jesus, Peter thought. He remembered his friend James. King Herod had persecuted him for being a Christian too. Soon after that Peter was arrested. He wondered what King Herod was up to.

At last Peter fell asleep, but he was restless and began to dream. In the middle of his dream a bright light shined into his cell.

Peter woke up and saw an angel standing in front of him. "Get up and get dressed," the angel said. Peter started to point out that the chains held him tight—but suddenly the chains dropped off. The angel led Peter past the guards and out of the prison.

The angel disappeared as quickly as it had come. Peter hurried to a house where he knew all his friends were praying for his safety. *I have to tell my friends about the miracle God did to keep me safe,* he thought. When the servant girl let him inside, Peter led the group in praising God.

Becoming a Man of God

A man of God prays for others.

What awesome friends Peter had! They stopped everything they were doing and prayed for him. Do you have a list of family members or friends for whom you pray? Do you know if there is someone praying for you? If so, how does that make you feel?

A Verse to Remember

So admit your sins to each other, and pray for each other so that you will be healed. Prayers offered by those who have God's approval are effective.

James 5:16

Shake and Break

Acts 16:16–40

The jailer shoved Paul into a dark cell in the very center of the prison. Paul had been in prison before, but this time he and Silas were in big trouble. The jailer had strict orders to make sure they didn't escape.

All I did was set a young girl free from the bad spirit that controlled her, Paul thought. *You'd think people would thank me for saving her.* Instead Paul and Silas were thrown into prison.

"Silas, the other prisoners here need to know that God loves them," Paul said.

"Right, and we have a captive audience," Silas agreed. They began singing songs and praising God. The prisoners listened to the words Paul and Silas sang.

Around midnight the walls and floor of the prison started shaking. Paul and Silas were tossed across the room, and the chains on their legs broke off. The cell doors broke open too. Prisoners got up to escape.

The jailer struggled through piles of stones to see his jail destroyed. Thinking all his prisoners were gone he began to panic. "Don't worry," Paul said. "We're all here."

The jailer was amazed that all the prisoners stayed when they could have escaped. "Sirs," he asked Paul and Silas, "can you tell me how to be saved?"

Becoming a Man of God

*A man of God knows others
are watching him.*

Paul and Silas could have escaped when the earthquake opened the prison doors. But they didn't because other people knew they were Christians. People were watching them to see how they behaved.

Do others see obedience to God when they look at how you behave?

A Verse to Remember

Don't let anyone look down on you for being young. Instead, make your speech, behavior, love, faith, and purity an example for other believers.

1 Timothy 4:12

Shipwreck

Acts 27:13–44

Paul knew there was no real reason for his arrest. The
only complaint against him was that he preached about
Jesus Christ.

"Move it!" the guard jabbed his spear at the line of prisoners filing onto the big ship. Chained together, the prisoners couldn't move quickly, but the guard paid no attention.

One morning a strong wind sent the sailors into a panic. "Storm coming; tie down the cargo! Move it!" They cracked whips across the prisoners' backs as they pushed to get set for the storm.

Paul heard the sailors say, "We're taking on water. The ship is going to go down."

The prisoners bailed water as fast as their chains would allow them to move, but the ship kept sinking lower. "Lighten the load. Throw over the cargo. Throw anything that's loose!" the sailors yelled.

"Stop worrying!" Paul shouted over the wind. "God told me in a dream that the ship will sink. But we will all be saved. Trust him!"

Later the ship hit rocks and broke into a million pieces, but every man on the ship—prisoners, sailors, and guards—made it safely to shore just as God said they would.

Becoming a Man of God

A man of God stays calm in a crisis.

The sailors and prisoners thought they were going to die. But Paul trusted God, and God said that he would take care of everyone on the ship.

What kinds of things make you afraid or nervous?

A Verse to Remember

Turn all your anxiety over to God because he cares for you.

1 Peter 5:7

The Holy City

Revelation 21

John was a friend of Jesus. He heard him teach and saw him do amazing miracles. He also saw Jesus die on the cross.

When John was an old man God sent an angel with a special message. John wrote it down in a book called Revelation.

John said this in his message:

The old world will disappear someday. A new city will come down from heaven and God's people will live in it with him. This city will sparkle like diamonds on a sunny day. Big walls will protect the whole city.

A new city will come down from heaven...

...and God's people will live with him.

Each side of the wall will have three gates. Each gate will be named for one of the twelve tribes of Israel and an angel will stand guard at each gate.

The wall of this city will have twelve big foundation stones, each named for one of Jesus's disciples.

The city will be made of pure gold. The foundation stones of the wall will have beautiful gemstones in them like emerald, onyx, topaz, and amethyst. The twelve gates will be made of pearls. Each gate will be one single pearl.

The Bible

My Bible

There will be no need for a sun or moon in this beautiful city, because God's light will fill it. Nothing bad will happen inside, and there will be no sadness.

John wrote about the holy city so that God's children can look forward to being there someday—with Jesus and everyone who loves him!

Becoming a Man of God

A man of God knows heaven is waiting for him.

It's exciting to think about being in heaven with God someday, isn't it? God has planned a beautiful place filled with love and complete happiness for his children.

Do you think about heaven? Do you know anyone who has already died and is with God now?

A Verse to Remember

Everyone who wins the victory will inherit these things. I will be their God, and they will be my children.

Revelation 21:7

Bible Stories for
Mothers & Daughters

WITH WHIMSICAL AND COLORFUL ILLUSTRATIONS, and a large, easy-to-read font, these Bible storybooks will encourage quality quiet time with Mom and instill in girls a love for the Bible at a young age.